alpha science

Light

Catherine Chambers

Evans Brothers Limited

This book is based on *Designs in Science Light* by Sally and Adrian Morgan, first published by Evans Brothers Limited in 1993, but the original text has been simplified.

Evans Brothers Limited
2A Portman Mansions
Chiltern Street
London W1M 1LE

First published 1997

Printed in Hong Kong

ISBN 0 237 51773 6

Managing Editor: Su Swallow
Editor: Catherine Bradley
Designer: Neil Sayer
Typesetting: TJ Graphics
Production: Jenny Mulvanny
Illustrations: Hardlines, Charlbury
                David McAllister

Acknowledgements

For permission to reproduce copyright material the authors and publishers gratefully acknowledge the following:

Cover Adrian Morgan, Ecoscene
Title page Will and Demi McIntyre, Science Photo Library
Contents page Sally Morgan, Ecoscene **page 4** NASA/Science Photo Library **page 6** Phil Jude, Science Photo Library **page 7** Philip Craven, Robert Harding Picture Library **page 8** Donald E Carroll, The Image Bank **page 9** (top) Agence Nature, NHPA (bottom) Adrienne Hart-Davis, Science Photo Library **page 10** Jany Sauvanet, NHPA **page 11** Sally Morgan, Ecoscene **page 12** Elyse Lewin, The Image Bank **page 13** (top) Robert Harding Picture Library (left, inset) Roger Tidman, NHPA (bottom) Sally Morgan, Ecoscene **page 14** (left) Adrienne Hart-Davis, Science Photo Library (right) Hans Reinhard, Bruce Coleman Ltd **page 16** (top and inset) Sally Morgan, Ecoscene (bottom) Dr Morley Read, Science Photo Library **page 17** Sally Morgan, Ecoscene **page 18** Adam Hart-Davis, Science Photo Library **page 19** (left) Malcolm Fielding, Science Photo Library (right) Amy Trustram-Eve, Science Photo Library (bottom) Anthony Bannierty, NHPA **page 21** (top) G.I. Bernard, NHPA (bottom) Ken Lucas, Planet Earth Pictures **page 22** Richard Kirby, Oxford Scientific Films **page 23** Sally Morgan, Ecoscene **page 24** (top) A Stewart, The Image Bank (bottom) World View/Bert Blokhuis, Science Photo Library **page 25** Hank Morgan, Science Photo Library **page 26** (top and middle) George Bernard, NHPA (bottom) Sally Morgan, Ecoscene **page 27** (left) Robert Harding Picture Library (bottom) Stephen Dalton, NHPA **page 28** Sally Morgan, Ecoscene **page 29** Sally Morgan, Ecoscene **page 31** (left) G.I. Bernard, Oxford Scientific Films (right) Sally Morgan, Ecoscene **page 32** Sally Morgan, Ecoscene **page 33** Dr Frieder Sauer, Bruce Coleman Ltd **page 34** (left) Sally Morgan, Ecoscene (right) Robert Harding Picture Library **page 35** Sally Morgan, Ecoscene **page 36** (top) Gerald Lacz, NHPA (bottom) John Murray, Bruce Coleman Ltd **page 37** (top and middle) Claude Nuridsany and Marie Perennou, Science Photo Library (bottom) Marcel Isy-Schwart, The Image Bank **page 38** (top) Sally Morgan, Ecoscene (bottom) James Holmes, Science Photo Library **page 39** (top) Jany Sauvanet, NHPA (bottom) McAlpine Helicopters Ltd. **page 40** (left) Robert Harding Picture Library (right) G.I. Bernard, NHPA **page 41** Sheila Terry, Science Photo Library **page 42** US Department of Energy/Science Photo Library **page 43** (top) Kim Steele, The Image Bank (bottom) Sinclair Stammers, Science Photo Library

Contents

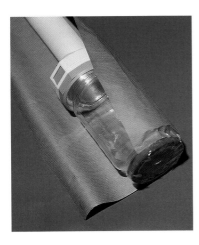

Introduction

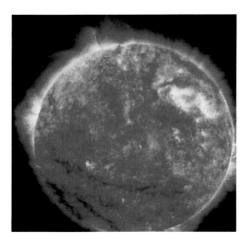

The sun is a ball of burning gases.

Light is a form of energy. Light energy is often given off by materials when they burn. The sun is a ball of burning gases which give off lots of light. Life on Earth depends on this light.

About 300 years ago, a scientist called Sir Isaac Newton studied light. He found that light travels in straight lines. He also found that light casts shadows. He knew that light bounces off mirrors, too. But he didn't know that light is made up of tiny packets of energy. These packets are called photons.

How light moves

The spectrum of light stretches from long radio waves to very short cosmic rays. Visible light is just a small part of the spectrum (look for the eye on the diagram). Wavelengths have different uses.

We now know that light also moves as waves, like ripples crossing a pond. The waves all travel at the same speed. This is 300,000 km every second!

Look at the wave diagram on page 5. The top of each wave is called a peak. The distance between two peaks is the wavelength. Light has different wavelengths. Light photons

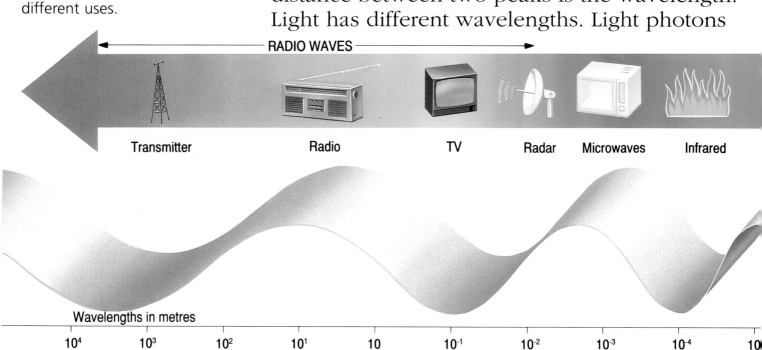

RADIO WAVES

| Transmitter | Radio | TV | Radar | Microwaves | Infrared |

Wavelengths in metres

| 10^4 | 10^3 | 10^2 | 10^1 | 10 | 10^{-1} | 10^{-2} | 10^{-3} | 10^{-4} | 10 |

with a short wavelength carry a lot of energy. Photons with a long wavelength have less energy. Look at the diagram below to see what the different wavelengths are used for.

Sunlight is a mixture of colours which appear white. The colours are made of different wavelengths of light. For example, red has long wavelengths. But blue has short wavelengths.

We do not see all the light given off by the sun. We only see red, orange, yellow, green, blue, indigo and violet. These are known as the visible spectrum. You can see the colours in a rainbow. We see a rainbow when sunlight passes through raindrops. The water bends the light and splits it into the seven colours.

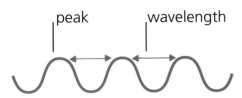

peak   wavelength

Invisible wavelengths

Look for the eye on the diagram. We can only see a few of the wavelengths of light. The ones we can see make up the 'visible spectrum'. The other wavelengths are invisible,

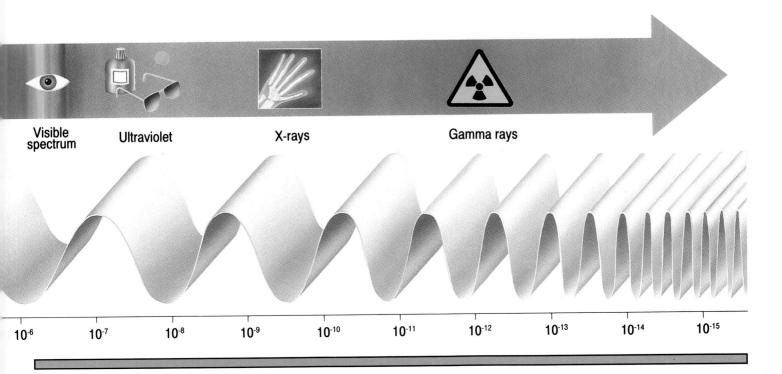

Visible spectrum   Ultraviolet   X-rays   Gamma rays

10^{-6} 10^{-7} 10^{-8} 10^{-9} 10^{-10} 10^{-11} 10^{-12} 10^{-13} 10^{-14} 10^{-15}

The longest wavelengths are radio waves. They are more than 1km long. But the shortest are gamma rays. They are less than 0.000000001mm long!

Measurement
In this book, some measurements are shortened:

Units of length
km kilometre
m metre
cm centimetre
mm millimetre

Units of temperature
°C degrees Celsius

Units of speed
km/h kilometres per hour
km/s kilometres per second
m/s metres per second

Units of area
ha hectare
cm² centimetre squared
mm² millimetre squared

Units of volume
cm³ centimetres cubed

Key words
Photon a tiny particle of light with a small amount of energy.
Spectrum the rainbow colours. They are made when white light is split by a raindrop or through specially shaped glass.
Wavelength the distance between two peaks.

White light bends as it passes through water. The white light breaks up into rainbow colours.

but we use them in many ways. The longest wavelengths have little energy. They are used in transmitters to pass on signals. Televisions and radios pick up the signals. This is how we get pictures and sound. The shortest wavelengths have lots of energy. They carry so much energy that they can be dangerous. They give out harmful radiation.

Each group of waves have different wavelengths. They each behave in a special way. The whole group is called the electromagnetic spectrum.

This book shows what light is and what it does. It also shows how light can be made and used. It explains how we see light and colour. As you read it, use the **Key words** boxes. These will explain difficult words. So will the **Glossary** on page 44.

When light hits an object

Transparent objects

Light usually passes through glass. But at certain angles it is reflected instead.

Transparent objects are clear. You cannot see them. This is because light passes straight through them. Air is transparent. Glass can be transparent, too. But sometimes light reflects off the surface making it difficult to see through the glass. Very shiny glass reflects a lot of light. When it does, you can see the glass itself.

Opaque objects

Translucent things, such as clouds, let some light through. Do you know any others?

Opaque objects don't let any light through. Most objects are opaque. They absorb, or soak up, some of the light. But they reflect, or bounce back, some light as well. We can see the object because we see the light reflecting from it. In the dark, we can't see things because no light reflects from them. Light can't pass through an opaque object. So there is a dark shadow behind it.

Translucent objects let some light through. But they scatter the rest of the light. Sunglasses are translucent.

Light hits the mirror and bounces off at the same angle.

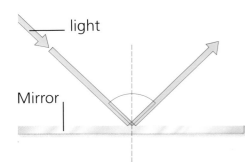

Mirrors

If you look in a mirror, you see your face. Light reflects off your face on to the mirror. The light bounces back off the mirror like a ball bouncing off the ground, and allows us to

Dentists use concave mirrors so that they can see the teeth more clearly.

! *The largest concave mirror in a telescope is 6m in diameter. It can pick up light from stars millions of kilometres away.*

? *How many types of concave and convex mirrors do you see around you?*

see the image.

If the mirror is flat, the images are the same size as the objects themselves.

But some mirrors are curved and this changes the size of the image. Outward, bulging curves are called convex. Convex mirrors make the image smaller than the object. They also reflect light from a wide area. Security mirrors in shops are convex. This is so that large areas of a shop can be seen.

Inward curves are called concave. These make the image bigger. Dentists use concave mirrors. They make the teeth look bigger. Some telescopes have huge concave mirrors. They can collect very faint light from far-off stars which we can barely see.

Animal mirror magic

The hatchet fish lives deep down under the sea. It has large silver scales on its sides which

EXPERIMENT

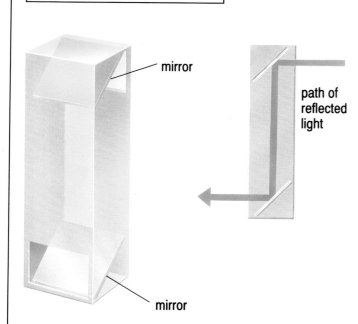

mirror

path of reflected light

mirror

Building a periscope

Periscopes are used on submarines. They let you see ships floating on the sea above. They are also used to see around corners. You can make a simple periscope of your own. You will need 2 small mirrors, some cardboard or a long tube, a pen, sticky tape and scissors. The diagram will show you how to make the periscope.

Can you answer these questions?:

● Does it matter how long the tube is?

● How could you improve the design of your periscope?

● Would painting the inside of the tube black help?

act like mirrors. They reflect back light from the water and help the fish to stay invisible. Other fish won't see it so it doesn't get eaten!

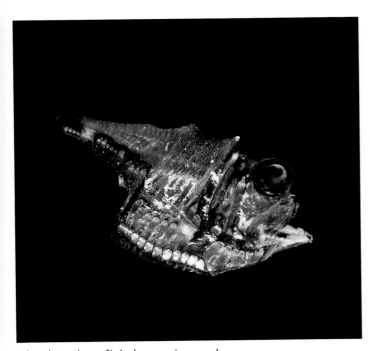

The hatchet fish has mirrored scales along the side of its body.

Seeing in the dark

The bushbaby is a nocturnal animal. It comes out at night. But how does it see in the dark? The bushbaby has huge eyes. They let in the maximum light. At the back of each eye is a mirrored layer. This layer reflects light back out of the eye, giving the bushbaby's eye a second chance to absorb the light.

Bending light

These objects in the water look bent. This is because of light refraction.

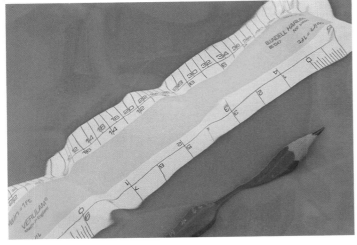

Light usually travels in straight lines. But sometimes it bends, or refracts. You can find this out for yourself. Take a drinking glass. Half fill it with water. Stand a pencil at an angle in the water. Look through the side of your glass. The pencil looks bent where it meets the water. Light bends when it travels from one clear substance to another. You have just proved it! Light bends because it travels at different speeds through the substances. It travels faster through air than water.

! *Light travels through space at 300,000km/s but only at 225,000 km/s through water.*

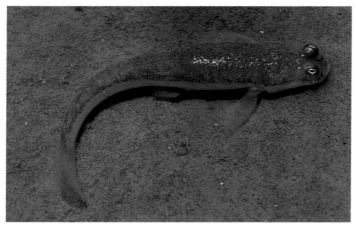

The four-eyed fish has eyes shaped for seeing above and below the water.

Using refraction

Lenses work by refracting, or bending, light. Spectacles, microscopes and telescopes use lenses. The light bends as it travels from the air to the plastic or glass of the lens. This can make objects look a lot closer than they really are.

Refraction is used in nature. The four-eyed fish swims along the surface of the water. It needs to see in the air and in the water. The four-eyed fish really only has two eyes, but each eye is divided into two halves. Each half is a different shape which makes the light refract differently in each half. The fish can see in the air with the top half and in water with the bottom half.

Refraction in optical fibres

 Optical fibres are much thinner than a human hair.

A beam of light bounces along the inner strand of an optical fibre, unable to escape.

beam of light

bundle of optical fibres

outer strands of glass

inner strands of glass

Optical fibres allow light to travel a long way. They also allow it to travel around corners. An optical fibre has two very long, thin strands of glass. One strand lies inside the other. Light moves along the inner strand. When light is shone into one end of the fibre, it travels along the inner strand. It can't escape until it reaches the other end. So light can be made to travel long distances and round bends.

Optical fibres are very useful for seeing things that are in difficult places. Doctors use them to see into

EXPERIMENT

Trapping light in a jet of water

You can make trapped light follow a curved jet of water. Then you will see how an optical fibre works. You will need a torch, a jam jar with a tight lid, a piece of brown paper 20cm x 20 cm and some sticky tape. You'll need to work over a sink. It's best to do this at night.

1 Make one large hole (0.5 cm across) in the centre of the jar lid. Then make a smaller hole (0.2 cm across) near the edge of the lid. Fill the jar with water. Then cover the holes with sticky tape.
2 Lay the jar on its side. Wrap the brown paper tightly around the jar in a tube shape. Stick the paper right down near the lid.
3 Push the torch through the paper tube behind the jar.
4 Turn the torch on so it shines through the water. Make sure no light escapes behind the torch or in front of the lid.
5 Darken the room.
6 Lay the jar on its side and hold it over the sink. Keep the small hole at the top.
7 Remove the tape from the holes using one hand.
Now watch the water escaping through the large hole. A beam of light is trapped in the jet as it pours out.

A block of ordinary glass just 1m thick is opaque. But the glass used to make optical fibres is very pure. You could through a block 1km thick!

the body without an operation. Engineers use them to see inside engines without having to take them apart. Telephone systems use optical fibres to carry messages over long distances.

Key words
Mirror a smooth polished surface that reflects light to form an image.
Refraction the bending of light rays as they pass from one substance to another.
Reflection a wave of light that bounces off an object.

Coloured light and pigments

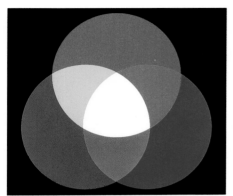

This colour wheel shows the three primary colours of light. It also shows how the three secondary colours are made.

Mixing coloured light

There are three main colours of light. These are red, blue and green. They are called the primary colours of light. If two primary colours are mixed together, they make a secondary colour. But it isn't like mixing paints together. Red and green paint make brown. But red and green light make yellow light. There are three secondary colours of light. These are yellow, cyan and magenta. In the diagram you can see white light in the middle. This is made by mixing all the primary colours of light together.

Filtering coloured light

Colours of light can be removed by using a filter. So, if white light is shone through a red filter, you will see only red shining through it. This is because the filter only allows red light wavelengths through (see page 4). It stops the other light colours. Cyan is made of green and blue light. So a cyan filter will let only these colours through. Filters are used in the theatre for special effects.

Humans can have skin of many different shades. Darker skin gives a bit more protection from the sun.

The ozone layer is a natural filter high above earth. It filters out some of the sun's invisible ultraviolet (UV) light (see page 5). UV light can damage our skin. But our skin is a light filter, too. It filters out some of the UV light that reaches us, stopping UV light from going too deep.

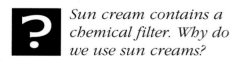

? *Sun cream contains a chemical filter. Why do we use sun creams?*

▷ Some tropical tree frogs have a filter in their skin to give them a green colour.

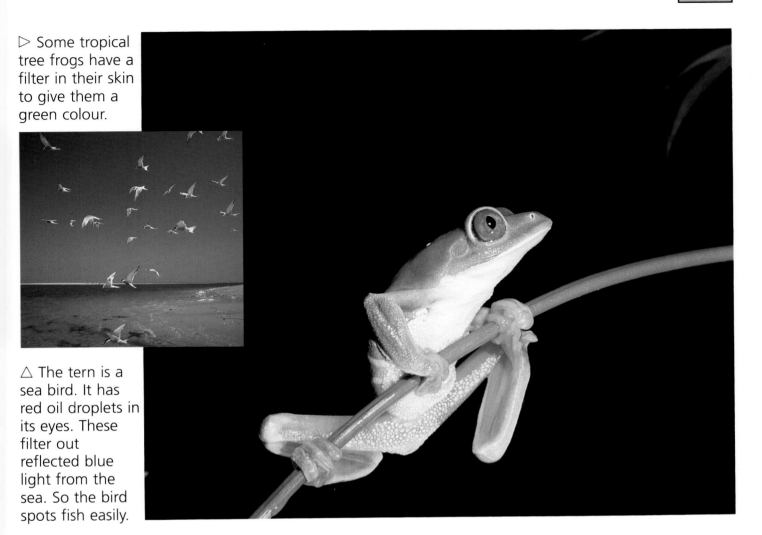

△ The tern is a sea bird. It has red oil droplets in its eyes. These filter out reflected blue light from the sea. So the bird spots fish easily.

EXPERIMENT

How colour filters work

See how colour filters work by making this filter box. You will need a shoe box, scissors, some sticky tape, green, blue and red cellophane, a torch and a some coloured objects.

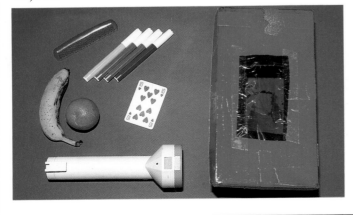

1 Cut out a rectangle from the shoe-box lid. Stick a piece of coloured cellophane over the hole.
2 Cut a hole in the end of the box. Make the hole the same size as the torch.
3 Put a coloured object in the box. Place the lid on the box.
4 Switch on the torch and look through the cellophane. What can you see?
5 Now put different coloured objects in the box. Look through the lid again. Which colours change? Which are the same?
6 Now change the colour of the cellophane. Look at all the objects again. What has happened?

Pigments

The cherry's red pigment absorbs all wavelengths of light except red ones.

The lemon's yellow pigment absorbs all wavelengths of light except red, yellow and green. These are reflected as yellow.

Pigments give all things their colour. They absorb some wavelengths of light and reflect others. Pigments are used to make paint. This book is coloured by pigments! There are three main, or primary, pigments. These are blue, red and yellow.

A lemon looks yellow. This is because it absorbs all the other light colours except red, yellow and green. Red and green light make yellow light, which is what we see.

Pigments in nature

Animals and plants can use their colour to attract attention, to warn off enemies or to help them hide.

The skin of an octopus has cells filled with different coloured pigments. The octopus can show how it feels by changing its colour. When the red cells are large, the octopus looks red. A red octopus is angry! The octopus has 35 colours. Scientists don't know what all the colours mean.

People need pigments to make paints and dyes. The first pigments were from the earth, plants and animals. Walnut skins give a rich brown colour. Bright red can be made by crushing a type of beetle!

Dyes can be made in all sorts of colours.

The pink colour of these flamingoes comes from a pigment in their food.

How a photograph is developed

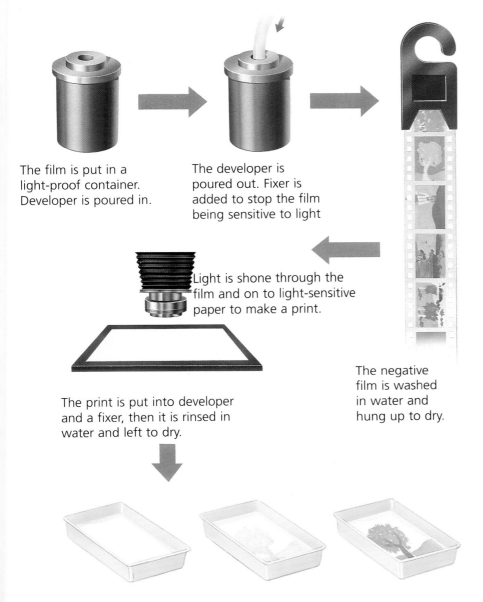

The film is put in a light-proof container. Developer is poured in.

The developer is poured out. Fixer is added to stop the film being sensitive to light

Light is shone through the film and on to light-sensitive paper to make a print.

The print is put into developer and a fixer, then it is rinsed in water and left to dry.

The negative film is washed in water and hung up to dry.

Black and white photographs are made with light. Photographic film and paper are very sensitive to light. This means they pick up light easily. The sensitive part of film comes from a chemical called silver bromide. Tiny grains of silver bromide are mixed with a transparent liquid. This is spread on to a strip of transparent plastic and left to dry.

When you take a photograph, photons of light hit the film. They change the silver bromide into silver metal. The brightest part of the picture is the darkest on the film. This is because more silver bromide gets hit by photons. So more silver is made. This is how you get film negatives. The brightest part of your picture looks really dark on the negative film. The darkest part looks quite pale.

The film has to be kept dark before a print is made from it. Look at the diagram to see how prints are made.

A beam of light is shone on to special paper. This paper is very sensitive to light. The dark areas of the negative won't let the light through easily. So they turn out white on the paper. The light areas will turn out dark. So, a white cloud will look black on the negative. But it will look white again on the printed paper.

Colour printing

Colour printing uses mixtures of the three secondary colours of light. These are cyan, magenta and yellow. Black is also used. Each coloured image has to be separated into the four colours, using filters. To print the final image, the colours are printed one on top of the other. Each print is made up of tiny dots of colour. You can see

To make a black and white print, a beam of light is shone through the negative (small picture) on to light-sensitive paper. The dark areas on the negative look light on the photograph.

Three images in cyan, magenta and yellow are put together with a black image to make a full colour picture.

The bottom picture was made using film sensitive to IR light. This is light we can't even see! (see page 4.) What has it done to the real picture on the right?

the printing dots if you look at a picture in this book through a strong magnifying glass.

Nowadays, an electronic scanner can pick out the colours of an image electronically. It is much quicker than using photographic separation. It is also more accurate.

? *Why is it safe to develop a black and white film in red light, but not in blue?*

Key words
Filter a transparent substance that only lets through light of certain wavelengths.
Pigment a substance that gives materials their colour. They absorb some wavelengths of light and reflect others.

Making light

This oxygen atom has a nucleus surrounded by a cloud of electrons.

Light is made when atoms are given energy. Atoms are the smallest part of any substance. Everything is made up of atoms. Look at the diagram of an atom. The ball in the middle is the nucleus. A cloud of electrons is whizzing all around it. When the electrons take in extra energy, from electricity, for example, they jump. They then let go of the energy. The energy they let go is given out as light energy. This is what we can see.

Electric lights

There are four main types of electric light. These are tungsten filament light bulbs, tungsten halogen bulbs, neon lights and fluorescent tubes.

The tungsten filament bulb has a tiny, thin metal strand inside it. This strand is called a filament. The filament is given electric energy. When this electricity flows through the filament, the filament glows a yellow-white colour.

Tungsten does not melt easily. So it's a good substance to use for a light bulb. But when it gets hot, it mustn't have air around it. The oxygen in the air makes the tungsten 'dissolve' away or evaporate. So the filament has a glass bulb wrapped around it. The bulb

At night our cities are lit up by thousands of coloured lights. These lights can be seen even from space.

On the right are two normal tungsten bulbs. On the left is a halogen bulb. All bulbs lose a lot of energy in heat.

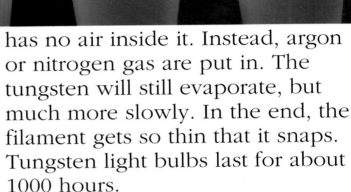

Neon lights are often used in advertising displays.

Which kinds of light do you use in your home? Do some use more energy than others?

The filament of a tungsten bulb reaches 2500°C.

has no air inside it. Instead, argon or nitrogen gas are put in. The tungsten will still evaporate, but much more slowly. In the end, the filament gets so thin that it snaps. Tungsten light bulbs last for about 1000 hours.

A different type of light bulb lasts for 2000 hours. But it is more expensive to make. It has halogen gas inside it. This makes the tungsten last even longer. The gas allows the filament to be heated to a high temperature. This makes it brighter than an ordinary tungsten bulb. But the extra heat makes an ordinary glass bulb melt. So the bulb is made of quartz glass instead.

Neon lights are tubes containing gas such as argon or neon. They have no filament. A strong electric current is passed through the gas. Together, the electricity and the gas usually give a red light. But new colours are now being created using different types of gas. Neon lights brighten our cities at night. They are often used for advertising.

Fluorescent tubes work in a different way. Each glass tube has a coating of a chemical

These yellow sodium lights are used to help plants grow.

powder inside it. The chemical is usually phosphor. The tube also contains mercury vapour. This is a kind of gas. When an electric current is passed through the tube, the mercury vapour gives off UV light. As we saw on page 5, UV light is invisible. But the phosphorous powder on the tube makes the UV light glow. It is a blue-white light. If sodium vapour is used instead of mercury, it gives a yellow glow.

Insects that light up

All living things give out light. We don't see it because it's infrared light (IR - see pages 4-5). But some living things give out light that we can see. When creatures make this light, it is called bioluminescence. But creatures do not use electricity to make light. They use chemicals inside cells in their body. The chemicals are changed and this creates light.

The female glow-worm is glowing to attract a mate.

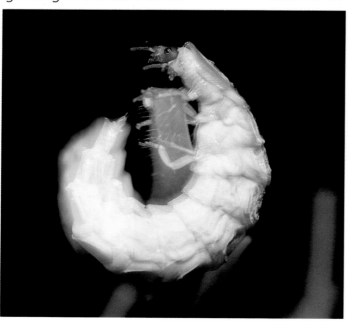

Most of the creatures that make light are insects that fly at night. They use the light to communicate with one another. Glow-worms and fireflies can produce a chemical called luciferin. The chemical glows when it mixes with oxygen. The oxygen is taken into the body from the air.

Perhaps the most exciting light shows are made by Malaysian fireflies. Here, only the male fireflies can make light. Hundreds of fireflies sit on the same bush in the swamps. Then, they all flash their light at the

This giant click beetle has two green lights behind its head and an orange light in its stomach.

? *Some night-flying insects use light to communicate. But what do moths use?*

Key words
Atom the smallest part of any substance.
Bioluminescence when light is given out by living things.

same time. The whole bush suddenly lights up - just for a second. The flash can be seen from hundreds of metres away. The female fireflies will easily find their partners.

Fish with light bulbs!

Many deep-sea fish make their own light. They use bacteria in their bodies. Bacteria are tiny single-celled organisms. Bacteria have many uses. Some help to rot or break down materials. Others can cause disease. But in the angler fish and the flashlight fish, bacteria glow. The angler fish has a bulb in front of its mouth. The bacteria in the bulb only glow when a lot of oxygen is added. This oxygen comes from the fish's blood. The fish can control the amount of blood pumping into the bulb. So the light can be switched off and on.

Scientists have copied the way creatures make light. Chemicals are shaken together to create green light. But it doesn't last long. So the lights are only used in an emergency – or for party fun!

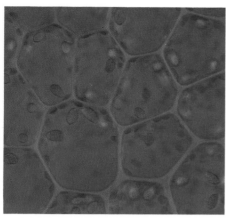

These leaf cells contain tiny round green discs packed with chlorophyll. The chlorophyll soaks up sunlight, which the plant uses to make food.

Oxygen made by the very first green plants killed many living things on earth.

The leaf is the site of photosynthesis.

Capturing light energy

The sun is like a huge power station which releases energy into space. But only a tiny fraction of this energy reaches the Earth in the form of light and heat. Much of this is reflected away from the Earth by the atmosphere. The remainder gets absorbed by the land, sea and air.

How plants use light energy

A small amount of the sun's light energy gets trapped by green plants. During the day, when it is light, plants use this energy to make their food. The food energy can be taken around the plant. So the plant can use it to grow. Or the plant can store the energy for the future.

Photosynthesis is the word we use to explain how plants make food. The word simply means, 'making something using light'. But the way plants make food isn't at all simple.

A plant leaf contains a green pigment called chlorophyll. The chlorophyll absorbs light which falls on the leaf. This energy fuels the food-making process.

The plant uses two other things to make food. The first is water. This is absorbed by the roots of the plant and taken up to the leaf. The second thing needed is a gas called carbon dioxide. This comes from the air and gets into the leaf through tiny holes.

The light energy combines the carbon dioxide and the water into food. The food is called glucose. The glucose

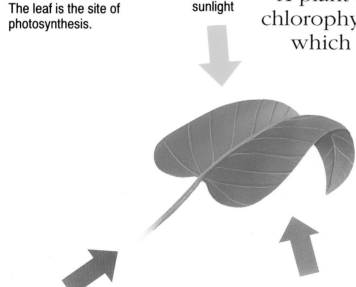

sunlight

carbon dioxide from air

water from roots

Almost all the oxygen in the earth's atmosphere has been made by green plants as they photosynthesise.

changes again into starch. This can be stored in the plant. When the leaf makes food, it makes oxygen at the same time. Some of this gas is used by the plant. But a lot of the oxygen leaves the plant and goes into the air, where it is used by animals.

The shape and thickness of leaves makes photosynthesis easy. Most leaves are flat, so they catch as much sunlight as possible. Many leaves can turn to the light throughout the day. They use a special stem to do this. It is called a petiole. A plant or a tree also spreads its leaves out so that as many leaves as possible can catch the light.

EXPERIMENT

Photosynthesis in action

When plants photosynthesise, they give out oxygen. If you look at pondweed, you can actually see this oxygen. It rises as bubbles through the water. Try collecting the bubbles. You will need some pondweed, a wide jam jar or clear measuring jug, a clear plastic funnel and a test tube.

1 Fill a sink with water. Put the jam jar upright in it. Let it fill with water.

2 Take a small amount of pondweed. Hold it down in the jam jars as you put the funnel over it.

3 Hold the test tube under the water and let it fill up. Keep it under the water as you move it over the end of the funnel.

4 Leave the jam jar in the sink. Pull out the plug and let the water drain away. You should be left with the jam jar, funnel and test tube full of water.

5 Lift everything out of the sink. Put it near the sun or in bright natural light. Now watch the bubbles rise from the pondweed. They will collect in the test tube. Watch how fast the bubbles rise.

6 Now do the experiment again. This time put everything in a darker place. Do the bubbles rise faster or slower? Does it take longer for the oxygen to collect in the test tube?

Solar panels and solar cells

Leaves are spread out so they catch as much sunlight as possible.

Solar panels trap heat from the sun. The heat is used to warm up water. Solar panels are flat and large. Like plant leaves, they are spread out flat so they can collect as much light as possible. The panels are placed so that sunlight falls on them for a long time.

Electricity can be made using solar cells. These have tiny layers of silicon in them. Silicon is a bit like transparent plastic. Light shines on the silicon and makes an electric current. When the light gets brighter, more electric energy is produced.

Solar power stations use heat and light from the sun to produce electricity for people to use at work and in their homes. Solar power is simple to produce and it does not pollute the atmosphere.

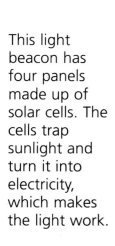

This light beacon has four panels made up of solar cells. The cells trap sunlight and turn it into electricity, which makes the light work.

The world's largest solar power station is in the Mojave Desert in California. The energy it produces could power 2000 homes.

Light energy can make gas

On a sunny day it is possible to make 100 litres of liquid hydrogen. This is enough to run a small car for a few days.

Key words
Photolysis breaking down water using the sun's UV light.
Photosynthesis when plants make food using light energy.

There have been many new discoveries using light. It has been known for a long time that heat energy excites atoms (see page 18). But it has now been found that light energy can excite atoms, too. This has been used to make hydrogen gas.

Hydrogen gas could be used as a fuel that produces very little pollution. There is lots of hydrogen in water. There is also oxygen. But it is very difficult to separate them out. Now, scientists have discovered that the sun's UV light (see page 6) can separate the hydrogen from the oxygen. This is called photolysis.

The process is very slow, though. So scientists have speeded it up by mixing the water with a blend of chemicals. The same chemicals can be used over and over again. It is hoped that large amounts of hydrogen can be made this way.

Sensing light

Most living things need to sense light. Many animals and plants sense the change in the amount of daylight throughout the year. Then animals know when to breed or to hibernate. Plants know when to flower or die down.

These crocus flowers open their flowers in the morning. They close them in the evening.

Plants and light

We know that plants need light to make their food (see pages 23-24). To make this easier, plant shoots grow towards the light. This is called phototropism.

The amount of light that a plant receives will affect its flowering. It is very important for plants to flower at the right time. Insects are sometimes needed to help make seeds inside the flower. If the flower opens at the wrong time, the insects won't be around to help.

The prayer plant's leaves spread out during the day. They fold upright at night.

Most flowers in Europe open in the summer, when the days are long. But others, like the chrysanthemum and the Christmas cactus, open later in the year, when the days are short. This is because they rely on different insects to pollinate them.

Some plants open their leaves during the

day, when it is warm. Then they close them at night. So the plants are protected from night frost. This type of reaction to light is called photonasty. Photonasty is very important for protecting the seed-making parts of plants, which are especially delicate.

Animals and light

Chameleons can change colour to fit in with the plants or rocks around them. Then their enemies won't see them. The brain sends messages to pigment cells in the skin. The cells then change their size. This makes different colours and patterns on the skin.

Scientists have used this idea to make a special glass. It is covered with a thin layer of a different material. When an electric current is passed through the material, it turns blue. This

△ Sunflower heads follow the sun as it moves during the day.

▷ The chameleon's skin can change colour to blend in with its background.

Can you think of any other animals that change colour? Why do they need to do this?

glass is called electrochromic. It is used for car wing mirrors because it helps reduce dazzle.

There are also new pigments that change colour when they get hot or cold. The pigments are thermochromic. They are used to make T-shirts that change colour. But they might soon be used on roofs. When the sun shines on the roof, the pigments get paler. This reflects the heat and keeps the building cool. When it is cooler and cloudy, the pigments get darker. They absorb more heat and make the building warmer.

Birds can sense the length of daylight. Some fly to warmer countries when the hours of daylight get shorter. In the spring, female birds recognise the longer, warmer days. They know that they should start finding partners and laying eggs. Animals such as hedgehogs sense daylight, too. This tells them when to hibernate for the winter.

These creatures probably use melatonin to sense daylight. Melatonin is a special type of chemical which is made in a tiny sac in the brain. When it gets dark, the melatonin travels around the body. It affects sleep. It also affects mating.

Melatonin can help humans. Sometimes we begin a long plane journey in daylight. We

In the spring, the feathers of the male mandarin duck are very bright. This helps to attract a mate.

EXPERIMENT

Flower clocks

Insects and bats soon learn when a flower will open. So they visit it at exactly the right time. *You* can tell the time of day by looking at

△ dandelion

water lily ▽

flowers. But first you have to study them. This is what the scientist, Carl Linnaeus, did in the 18th century. He showed how flowers could be used as clocks.

Do this experiment in the summer when there are lots of flowers. You will need to get up early and study the flowers for the whole day. Write down which flowers open early. Note down the time they open. Write down when they close, too. Don't forget that some flowers open in the evening.

For the next few days, just go out a few times during the day. Check the opening time of certain flowers. Then check the closing time. If the times stay the same, you can use these flowers as a clock. Look out for certain flowers - dandelion, passion flower, carnation, scarlet pimpernel, hawkbit, bindweed, water lily and evening primrose.

Now check the same flowers in different weathers. What happens on a cold or wet day?

Key words
Phototropism when a plant's shoot grows towards the light.
Thermochromic when colour changes in different temperatures.

expect it to be dark when we land. But often, we still land in daylight! This is because of time changes from one area to another. Moving through these time zones makes the body tired. This is called jet lag. Some scientists think that melatonin tablets help the body to feel normal again. Others think that sitting under bright lights helps cure jet lag.

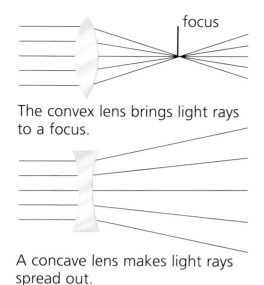

The convex lens brings light rays to a focus.

A concave lens makes light rays spread out.

Seeing with light

An eye, a camera and a magnifying glass share two things. First, they all work best in the light. Second, each has a convex lens. It is shaped like a bulge (see page 8). When light shines through it, a small upside-down image is made. A convex lens bends rays of light so that they come together. You can see this in the diagram. The place where they meet is the focus. Here, the image is sharp and you can see it clearly. The image is blurred where the rays do not meet.

The eye

Short-sighted people cannot see in the distance. This is because the image falls in front of the retina. What lens shape would correct this?

The eye of fish, amphibians, reptiles, birds and mammals is almost round and contains several layers of cells. The eye's lens can change shape. This helps it to focus on objects both near and far away. Look at the diagram of the eye as you find out how the eye works.

Light bends as it passes through the clear cornea. The cornea helps to focus the light through the lens. The lens bends the light again. This focuses the light sharply on to the retina. The retina is the light-sensitive layer at

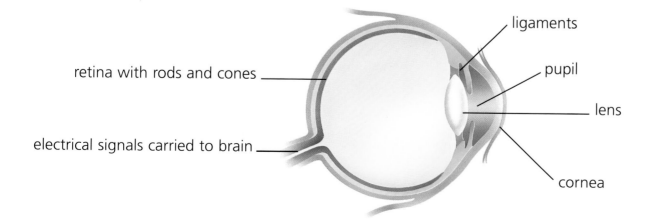

retina with rods and cones

electrical signals carried to brain

ligaments

pupil

lens

cornea

the back of the eye. If the light is focused sharply, so is the image.

The lens has to change shape to see things at different distances. If the eye is looking at a far-off object, the lens only needs to bend the light a little. So the lens has to be long and thin. But if the eye is looking at something close up, the lens needs to bend the light more. So the lens has to be short and fat. The shape of the lens is controlled by muscles and stringy ligaments attached to it.

Rabbits can see all around them with eyes at the side of their head. They need to watch out for foxes. Owls are hunters. Their eyes are at the front. This helps them to see small animals clearly.

 The eyes of the net-casting spider are 19 times more sensitive to light than the human eye.

Seeing an image

Light gets focused through the lens and on to the retina. This light-sensitive layer has two types of cell - rods and cones. There are a lot of rods. These enable us to see in black and white, and in the dark. There are less cones. But these let us see in colour. When light falls on the retina it excites the rods and cones. They send messages to the brain. The image is formed upside-down on the retina but the brain turns it round the right way.

Seeing colours

The cone cells in the retina are sensitive to red, green and blue light. When the cones act

EXPERIMENT

Controlling light in the eye

Too much light in the eye can damage the retina. So light is controlled by the pupil. This is a small hole in the eye. You can see it on the diagram on page 30. When there is a lot of light, the pupil gets smaller. So less light enters the eye. When the light is dim, the pupil gets bigger. So more light can enter. This helps the eye to see better in the dim light. Now watch your pupil change size!

You will need a small, flat mirror and a small torch.

1 Hold the mirror so that you can see your eye in it.

2 Switch on the torch. Hold it just behind and to the side of the mirror. Let the light shine near your eye, but *not* right in it!

3 Watch your pupil in the mirror. What happens to the size of the pupil? What happens when you switch off the torch?

! *Frogs' eyes are very sensitive to blue. In times of danger, they jump towards an area of blue. This is usually a safe pool of water!*

together, the eye sees all colours of the spectrum (see page 5). But the cones only work in the light. At night, the rods work on their own. So we can only see in black and white.

Birds see colours better than other animals. They have five types of cone. And each cone has a tiny light filter made of oil. With these two things, birds can see a huge range of colours and shades.

Some people cannot tell the difference between red and green. How will this be a problem in their lives?

Even these tiny plants, called algae, are sensitive to light. Each plant swims towards the light using two beating hairs.

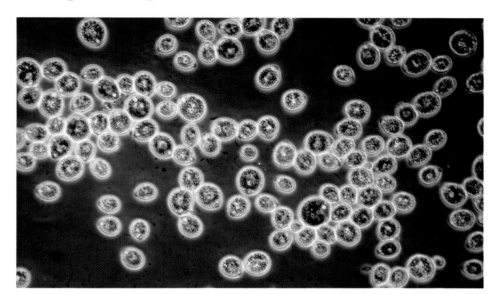

Even these simple plants seem sensitive to light.

Cameras

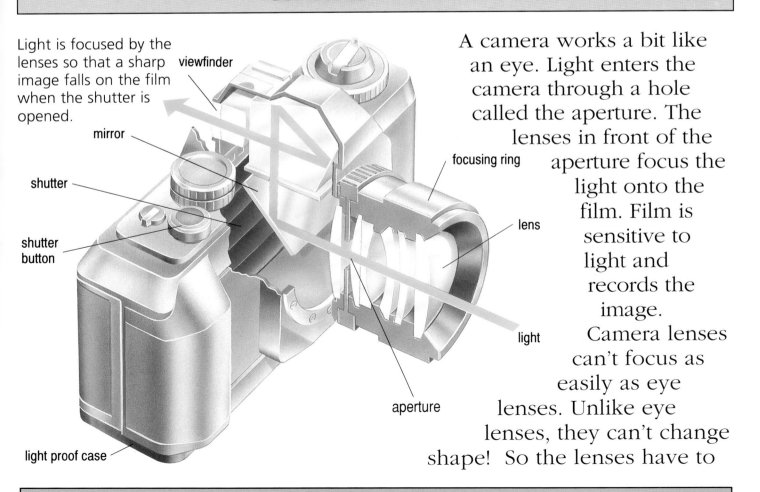

Light is focused by the lenses so that a sharp image falls on the film when the shutter is opened.

viewfinder

mirror

shutter

shutter button

focusing ring

lens

light

aperture

light proof case

A camera works a bit like an eye. Light enters the camera through a hole called the aperture. The lenses in front of the aperture focus the light onto the film. Film is sensitive to light and records the image. Camera lenses can't focus as easily as eye lenses. Unlike eye lenses, they can't change shape! So the lenses have to move backwards or forwards. Some cameras can do this automatically. On others, the photographer turns the focusing ring to make the image clear.

At this point, the film would be spoiled if light reached it. So there is a shutter between the film and the aperture.

When the picture is taken, the shutter lets the right amount of light through to the film. In bright light, the shutter is made to open for a short time. In dim light, it opens for a long time to let enough light in. You can find out how the film is turned into a picture on pages 15-16.

Television cameras have thousands of light senors. These are tiny picture cells - or pixels. An electric signal is made in each pixel when light falls on it. A scanner in the camera reads

! *There are about half a million pixels on a television screen.*

? *How are concave and convex lenses used all around us?*

△ The television screen is covered in rows of tiny dots, or pixels. Each row is either red, green or blue.

▷ A TV camera also uses pixels. Light on the pixels makes electrical signals, which can be broadcast all around the world.

EXPERIMENT

Making a pinhole camera!

Try making this simple camera. You will be able to see an image through it. But there is no film to record the image.

You will need a cardboard tube, no wider than 10cm, a pin, greaseproof paper, cooking foil, rubber bands and a pair of scissors.

1 Stretch cooking foil over one end of the tube. Stretch greaseproof paper over the other end. Hold them in place with the rubber bands.

2 Make a very tiny hole in the foil with the pin.

3 Place an object on the window sill. Turn off any lights in the room. Now hold the foil end of the camera towards the window.

4 Keep the camera still and look at the back end of the tube. What do you see? Which way up is the image?

5 Now do the experiment again. Make the pin hole larger. What happens to the image?

 The nautilus is a kind of sea snail. Its eye is just like a pinhole camera. There is no lens, only an opening and a retina.

the signals and sends a message down a long cable. All the messages are used to make up the picture.

The picture signals can be picked up by a television set. The television set has the same rows of pixels as the camera. Each pixel can be made to glow. The eye can be fooled into seeing many colours. If a red pixel glows near a green pixel, the eye will see yellow (see page 12). If a blue pixel glows near a green pixel, the eye will see cyan, and so on. The lines of pixels are scanned very quickly. Lots of images can be screened every second. This gives a continuous moving picture.

Key words
Convex curved outward in a bulge.
Concave curving inward like a bowl.
Focus the point where light rays meet.
Lens A curved transparent substance that bends light rays.

A goldfish can see both UV and IR light wavelengths.

Invisible light

We can't see all wavelengths of light. Some wavelengths are very short and they carry too much energy for us to see. UV is one of these wavelengths (see pages 5-6). Others are much longer and are too weak to see. Infrared is invisible.

The dangers of UV light

UV light cannot be seen, but it is very powerful. Sunlight carries a lot of UV light, which can be reflected from water and white surfaces such as snow.

UV light is dangerous to our eyes. It can damage the retina (see pages 30-32). The reflected light from snow can cause snow blindness. So people in snowy areas of the world need to protect their eyes.

The snow reflects dangerous UV light. Climbers have to wear darkened goggles to protect their eyes.

UV light can come from some artificial lights as well as the sun. It can spoil paintings. Oil paints darken and watercolours fade. UV can even weaken the threads in silk cloth. In the end, the threads will break.

The problems of UV light have increased in recent years. This is because more UV light is getting through the ozone layer around our Earth. Ozone is very good at absorbing UV light, but pollution has damaged the ozone layer. More and more people are suffering from eye problems and skin cancer because more UV light is reaching the Earth.

The yellow potentilla flower (above) looks very different in UV light (right).

Using UV light

Humans cannot see UV light. But honey bees can! Many flowers reflect UV light from their petals. This attracts bees, which feed on the nectar and pollen inside the flowers. At the same time, the bees pollinate the flowers. Bees see some of the colours that we see, too, but they can't see red.

Some chemicals, minerals and living things glow when UV light hits them. They give out fluorescent light. You can see the fluorescent light on the coral in this picture.

Scientists have used this idea to make white clothes look even brighter. Washing powders now contain chemicals that fluoresce in UV light. The chemicals stick to natural materials such as cotton. In sunlight, the washed white cotton looks a dazzling blue-white colour.

Some types of coral can fluoresce when UV light hits them.

EXPERIMENT

The honey bee's favourite colour

Find out the honey bee's favourite colour. Then train them to find a particular colour. Do this in the garden or on a balcony in warm sunny weather. You will need some squares of different coloured card - like the ones in the picture. You will also need some small clear dishes or lids and some sugary water.

1 Lay the coloured cards out close to each other. Place the dishes on top. Put a little sugary water in each. Now watch to see which colour the bees are attracted by.

2 For the next few days, put the sugary water only in the dish on the blue card. The bees should flock to this card.

3 Then one day, don't put sugary water into any of the dishes. Now watch the bees again. They should all still fly to the blue card, hoping for food.

Invisible infrared light

Hot objects give out invisible infrared light. When materials become *very* hot, they give out visible light.

Nearly every living thing gives out infrared (IR) light. So do very hot objects. But we can't see this light. This is because its wavelengths are too weak. You will see on pages 4-5 that IR wavelengths are even longer and weaker than those of the colour red. Red is the weakest colour wavelength that we can see.

When materials become very hot, the light wavelengths they give out become shorter and stronger and we start to see this light. It makes things look 'red hot'.

Using IR light

Many animals can detect IR light. The piranha fish is a fierce hunter that lives in the Amazon River. The waters are too murky to see much light. But the piranha fish can see the IR light. This light comes from the bodies of other fish and mammals in the water.

Scientists have made searchlights and goggles that can detect IR light. These are very useful for seeing in the dark. They are often used by soldiers. Military aircraft use IR light at night, too. One of these IR systems is called Forward Looking Infra-Red (FLIR). The system has a huge lens. It collects and focuses IR light on to sensors. The sensors then put the results on a screen. The airforce pilot can then see what objects might be in the way of the aircraft or helicopter.

These sensors are now helping other pilots. Pilots cannot see through fog and rain when the plane is on the ground. This is because the usual instruments only work in the air. But IR sensors help to guide the plane through bad weather on the ground.

Scientists are also developing tiny antennae that sense IR light. The antennae are like the sensors on an insect's head. They can detect IR light from gases such as carbon dioxide, which are responsible for global warming.

The piranha fish can see infrared light. It can hunt its prey in dark waters.

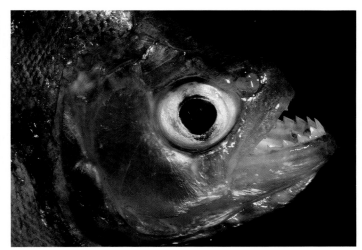

Key words
Fluorescence when a substance gives out light when it is hit by invisible UV light.
Infrared weak, invisible wavelengths of light.
Ultraviolet (UV) strong invisible wavelengths of light.

The FLIR system is used in police helicopters. It helps find people in the dark, or hiding.

When light waves meet

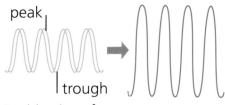

peak

trough

Positive interference creates a deeper colour.

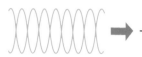

Negative interference cancels out the peaks and troughs, giving darkness.

Light waves move up and down in peaks and troughs. You can see this in the diagram. Sometimes, the peaks of different light waves meet exactly. This means that their troughs meet, too. Together, they make a richer, deeper colour. This meeting of waves is called positive interference. But sometimes, the peak of one wave meets the trough of another. They cancel each other out, creating darkness. This is called negative interference. Many patterns and colours can be made when light waves meet in different ways.

Interference patterns

Many insects have brilliant colours. The colours seem to change as you look at them from a different angle. This is caused by light waves interfering with each other.

The pits on the compact disc and the butterfly's wing make shiny rainbow-like patterns.

Butterfly wings often have a shiny rainbow appearance. The coloured patterns are made by tiny scales on a butterfly's wings. Many of these scales have no colour in them at all. But each scale has a bumpy surface made of ridges and furrows. When the light hits them, it scatters. The light waves move in all directions. When they crash into each other, different colours are made.

If you look at the surface of a compact disc,

the same thing happens. Rainbow colours are made by tiny pits in the surface. These scatter the light. Bands of rainbow colours can be seen in a soap bubbles. These are also made by interference, but in a slightly different way.

Polarised light

Polarised light shows up stress points in plastics. Coloured bands show where the stresses lie.

A light bulb gives out light waves that vibrate in different directions. But polarised light waves vibrate in just one direction. Polarised light can be made by passing ordinary light through a filter.

Polarised light has many uses. Polarising sunglasses cut down the glare from shiny surfaces. But they only work at the right angle. If you look straight down into water in bright light, polarising sunglasses allow you to see into the water. If you then lift your head up and look down at the water, the glasses won't work properly.

Polarised light is useful in engineering. It can help to find faults or stress in plastics. Polarised light is shone through the plastic. The light gets reflected from any bumps, ridges or cracks in the plastic. The reflected light can be seen as bands of coloured light.

! *The waterboatman is an insect that lives on the surface of ponds. Its eyes actually make polarised light stronger! This makes it easy to find water from the light reflecting off it.*

? *Why do photographers use polarising filters on their cameras?*

Key words
Interference when light waves meet together.
Polarised light wavelengths of light that vibrate in one direction only.

Light in the future

Light is exciting. Scientists are learning about light all the time. They are always finding new uses for light, too.

New lighting

There is always a need to find cheaper and better forms of light. Light bulbs need to be more efficient and lose less heat energy. Fluorescent bulbs are already better than ordinary light bulbs.

But scientists are now working on a very unusual light bulb. The light bulb is coated inside with a phosphor chemical. There is a coil in the centre of the bulb. This coil gives out invisible radio waves. The waves excite a vapour inside the bulb, which then gives out UV light, which is also invisible. The UV light then reacts with the phosphor chemical to create light. These bulbs will last about 14 years!

Compact fluorescent bulbs use much less electricity than tungsten bulbs.

Laser light

Lasers are thin beams of light. They can travel a long way without spreading out. The light waves of lasers are all the same length. All the waves' peaks lie together. So do all the troughs (see pages 40-41). It is a very strong, pure light. Powerful lasers can focus a fine beam of strong light on to one spot.

Lasers are used to cut through metals. Surgeons also use laser light in operations. Laser light is going to be used more and more

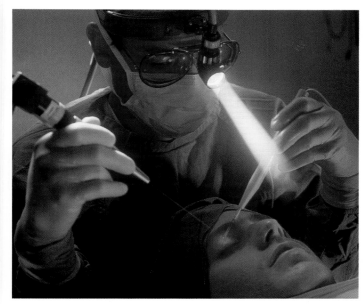

Laser beams can be finely controlled. So they are very useful in surgery. They are used in delicate eye operations. They also cut through blocked arteries.

in computing. It will also help in communications.

Lasers will soon be used in photography, too. The image will no longer be stored on a film. It will be on a compact disc (CD) instead, which will be read by a laser. This type of photography is known as digital photography.

Plants for the future

Farmers and flower growers now know how to control light in greenhouses to help fruit and vegetables to ripen at the right time and plants to flower at the right time. Controlling the amount of light and heat that plants get can also reduce the time it takes for plants to grow. Now, four crops of wheat can be grown in one year. Some types of cabbage, broccoli and turnip grow fully in just 36 days when they are grown under fluorescent light.

Light and us!

How else can light help us? The ancient Egyptians studied how colours can help cure sick people. Some of these lost secrets are now being used in chromotherapy. This treats people using different wavelengths of light.

There are many more exciting ways in which light can be used just waiting to be discovered. Scientists will probably find some of these ways by exploring the natural world still further.

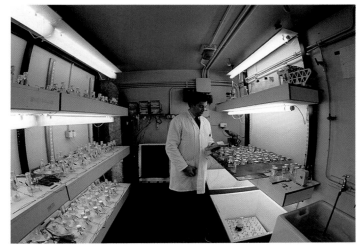

The light in this growth chamber can be controlled to help plants grow quickly.

Glossary

bacteria tiny, single-celled organisms
chlorophyll a green pigment in plant leaves that soaks up light
chromotherapy using light wavelengths to treat illness
electrochromic glass glass that changes colour when an electric current is run through it
film negative photographic film showing dark areas where there are pale ones in real life - and pale areas where there are really dark ones
filament a very thin wire of metal inside light bulbs
laser a thin, strong beam of light
melatonin a chemical in the brain that affects sleep
neon light tubes containing neon or argon gas
opaque describes objects that do not let light through
optical fibres strands of glass that allow light to travel along them
petiole a plant stem that bends towards the light

photolysis a process that uses UV light to separate gases
photonasty when flowers react to light by opening during the day and closing up at night
pixels tiny picture cells that light up to give a picture on a television screen
primary colours for light, these are red, green and blue
secondary colours for light, these are yellow, magenta and cyan
solar power power obtained from the sun's energy
silver bromide a chemical spread on photographic film
translucent describes objects that let some light through
transparent describes objects that let most light through
tungsten a metal used as a filament in light bulbs

Index